Queen of Kings Empress Nyajesus Nyayecu Elect of God of the Kingdom of Canaan United Afro States Southern Sudan Wakanda

Hebrew Israelites True Biblical History Origin

NYAJESUS REBECCA DUEN KOK TUNGKERNYANG MENELIK II

DEDICATION

I would like to dedicate my book to God, who is my Enteral Rock and my Redeemer, who of all my blessings flow, and my father, Prince Paul Duen Kok Tungkernyang Menelik ii and my mother, Her Majesty Queen Mary Nyegony Deng, for their wonderful love and support.

ACKNOWLEDGMENTS

I am very thankful for all my family and friends for the wonderful support and love they showed me over the years and I am very excited and blessed to have them in my life. May God bless all of you. Hallelujah, Amen, praise the Lord Inono.

Contents

The Miracles and Troubles of My Life Story

by Nyajesus Duen:

At the age of 4, God gave me a revelation of the four winds in my vision. At night, I saw a vision that scared me so much, and the next morning, I had no idea who to tell it to and if I do are they going to believe me? So I kept it to myself, but as my life was going on, the vision was still in my mind, and it still made me feel so afraid, and as a 4-year-old girl, I was thinking and saying to myself, what I am going to do? The vision changed my life, and I cannot live my life anymore without thinking about this vision. In my vision of the four winds, I saw a big wind that was blowing so strongly, and it was a dusty wind, and then I saw my dad going through the wind; I looked at him until he disappeared into the wind. But the wind was still bellowing, and I saw my sister, Sarah Nyapak Duer. And she was going through the wind the same way my dad was going, and I looked at her until she was gone through the wind. I looked, and I saw my brother Moses Buay Duer, and he was going through the wind, and this time I wanted to go too, but the wind did not let me go, and I saw my brother Moses walking through the wind like 'it was normal, I begin to cry and fight very hard for me to go through the wind because I want to go wherever my family is going, but the wind was so strong against me, and it 'didn't let go through, so I watch my brother Moses until he disappeared through the wind, and then the wind stops. Then I heard some people singing. I turned around, and I saw them standing beside the Nile River, gathering and singing a beautiful song. I looked at them until the song was finished, and then they stopped singing. But the wind came back, and this time, it was bellowing, much strong than before. I saw the trees, home, people, and everything being blown away, and there was thundering and lightning, and there was a loud noise. I see the whole world is in trouble. Then I woke up.

Two days later, when I had my first vision, I went to sleep, and I began to have a dream, and in my dream, my family and I moved to a new city, and in that new city, I saw people, and they were coming to our city, and there was a big war. I saw people running and many people being killed. I saw my family, and I was running, and I was crying. I saw people with big guns and shooting people and everything; it's so terrible. Thank I wake up. I was shaking so much, and I was very scared. I do not know what to do or who should I tell this dream, and I am only 4 years old. I just had a vision about four winds two days ago, and now I have this terrible dream. I said God, what's happening to me? I got up, and I went and took a bath, and I was thinking and saying to myself it's nothing; it was just a dream, and everything was going to be fine. So I went and played with my friends and tried to just forget about it. But the vision and the dream cannot go away from my mind. I was still thinking about them, and it made me feel so afraid.

Three Months later, me and my family were sitting down at our kitchen table eating lunch, and my dad began to tell us, he said, the time had come now for us to move to the city where my sister and her family lived. I cannot believe it. That's what I saw in my dream three months ago. Said oh, no, could that dream be true? And I began to feel so afraid, and my body began to shake very much. I got up and left the table because I 'didn't want any of my family to know what was happening to me, and maybe they could ask me about it. Icould not really explain it to them because I was not sure whether my vision and dream were real or not. I do know that I was only a 4-year-old who had never had any dream or a vision before, so I had no idea what to do. I was very confused.

A week later, me and my family moved to a new city in February of 1984, and I was thinking about the dream and the vision that I saw three months ago; I thought to myself, God, did you really give me a revelation? But then I said no, we moved, but maybe it's not to fulfill my vision and dream. So I moved on with my life in the new city with my family, and tried to forget it never happened.

The 1st Wind Blow

About a month later, we heard some news that the South Sudanese army was preparing to come and fight with us. When I heard that, my vision and dream I had about four months ago came back to my mind, and my body began to shake, and my heart began beating very hard in my chest; I felt so afraid. I hear my dad saying, why would the South Sudanese come to our city to fight us? What did we farmers ever do to them? And when I heard that, I said to myself, no, they will not come, and my terrible dream will not come true. So I got up and went to play with my friend, and I tried to forget about it, but the thought about my vision and dream did not go away.

About two weeks later, we heard some fighting in the city near our city, and the people in my city were saying, are those South Sudanese Army going come here and fight us too? For a month, they continued fighting cities, and our men had a meeting. they said that we were going to go and guard our city every night to protect our family. And they all agreed and began to go out every night and guard our city, but the South Sudanese did come, but we still heard news about them planning to come to fight with our people in our city. Then our men say that we have to let the children and the women leave our city and go to those other cities that are safe, and then we men will stay here and wait for those South Sudanese armies; if they come, we will fight them without our women, and children. All men agreed, and we women and children began to leave our city every night, and in the morning, we would come back to our city. When our men saw that there was no sign of those armies coming and fighting us, they said, okay, you women and children, don't leave the city anymore; maybe those South Sudanese armies will not come, but we will still go out every night to guard our city. So, the women and the children did not leave the city. On Saturday, January 29, 1985, Ethiopian officials came to our city and had a meeting with our men of the city. they said to them, we have heard that you have been going to our side of your city to guard it at night because you think that South Sudanese will come to fight you her, we want you to know that we have not let them come here, and fight with you in your city, so don't go out tonight, and guard your city. My dad was the one who was the interpreter at the meeting, and he said to his men, guys, these Ethiopian, what they are talking about us not going out tonight to guard our city is not a good idea, and think that they come here with different agenda. We do not need to listen to them; we have to go out tonight and guard our city to protect our families or our women, and children will the city, and for them to be safe. The men say my Dad, Paul Duer, and these Ethiopians said that those South Sudanese will not come here to fight us because they will not let them come to our city, and now you are saying we still have to go out tonight and guard our city? We are very tired of going out every night to guard our city, and tonight, we will stay home with our family and get a good night's sleep. While my dad was at the meeting, my big sister Sarah Nyapak Duer went to the Nile River to get some water, and when she came back home, she said to our mother, Mom, I saw some army with guns and army cars at the Nile River this afternoon when I went to get some water, and our mother said to her

I think that they are Ethiopian Army, but Sarah said to our mom no they are our South Sudanese soldiers. While my mother and my sister were speaking, our dad came home from the meeting, and he said at the meeting, the Ethiopian official told us that they came here to let us know that we do not need to be afraid anymore, for they will not let the South Sudanese soldiers come to our city to fight with us here, and they told us that we have to not go out tonight, and guard our city we have to stay with our family tonight and have a goodnight sleep. But I said to our men that we could not listen to these Ethiopian officials, and we have to go out as always and guard our city to protect our family, but they disagreed with me, and now they are not going out to guard the city tonight. My mom said to him Paul, Sarah went to the Nile River this afternoon, and she just was saying that she saw some soldiers with guns and cars, and she thought that they were the South Sudanese Army. My father said Mary, you have to leave now with our children; we are going to have a war, but I will not go with you because I cannot leave our people. But we said to our mother and our father we would not leave without your dad; you have to come with us, or we are not going, and maybe there is no war coming to our city. So, at that point, we just let it go, and that night, we went to sleep thinking that what the Ethiopian official said was true.

On Sunday morning at 5:am, January 30, 1985, our church elder, David, and his brother got up and went to seek his cow that was lost, and while they were walking to a city near our city, they saw something that looked like a tree outside our city, and they know that we do not have any trees on that other side before. They walk closer to that thing to see what it is, and they realize that they are soldiers and we have a war now. They ask themselves what are we going do now all our people are still sleeping? Elder David said to his brother, we have to wake our people up, but how? If we fire a gun, that Army will know that we know about them, and if we don't, they will soon kill our people while they are still sleeping. Then Elder David fired his gun, the soldier heard it, and the people woke up. When the soldiers realized that we woke up, they began to fire their guns into our city and came to us. Me and my family woke up and began to run to the bush outside our city, and the people were crying and running; when I saw that my dream came back to my mind, and I knew that this was my dream. The soldiers boomed at us and destroyed our homes. We went to a different city far away, and we have been running for 6 hours in the hot Sun from 6:am to 4:pm without water or food. Lost almost everything, and many of our people have been killed. But when we left our city earlier in the morning, our father was at our farmhouse where our cows were to protect them by opening the farmhouse and letting them go out so they could run away. I felt so sick, and I was thinking and saying they were going to kill my dad. At about 12 pm, my dad came, and when I saw him, I was very happy, and I thanked God for saving his life. Now we are in this new city trying to get some water and some food, but the people in this new city are so afraid now because of how terrible we look and the news they are hearing about the war that happened in our city. My mother said to us let's go to my sister's home, where my mother and your grandmother are, and we will have a rest there. So we go, and stay for the night there. The next morning, we woke up, and I was feeling so tired, and my feet were covered with bruises from running without shoes for 6 hours. At 7 am, we heard that people were leaving this city and going to other far cities because they were afraid, and they thought that the South Sudanese army was coming to fight with them here, too. So my dad said to my mother take the children with you, and I will come after you, but now I must go back to our city and see if there are any cows or anything left from us so I can bring them for our children. My mother said no, Paul, please don't go back there, just come with us now. But my dad left and went. We began to walk, and it was the hardest thing ever. My feet hurt, and my little sister Martha was only 2 years old. My mom had to carry her, and no one was going to carry me because my dad went back to look for our things.

Has a 6-year-old girl. I thought that I was very confused, and I realized that all these things happened because of my dream that I saw at 4 years old. That evening, we got to a town, and there were so many people there who were running away from the war; we sat down and tried to relax, and then we heard something that sounded like a boom, and we began to run outside the town, but the people said that it's okay there is no boom. We turned and saw our father's family city, and my brother Moses Buay and my sister Sarah Nyapak began to dance and said to our mother, please let's go there; Dad would follow us there. Our mother said okay, let's go, and then we went. We got there, and the people saw us, and they were very happy.

Two weeks later, our father came, and I was happy to see him; I love him very much, and he always treats me so special. Life seemed to go well with us, but a month later, in March of 1985, the South Sudanese followed us, and the war started again. Now it is even worse than the war we had about a month ago because now we are between two armies who are both enemies. The Northern Sudan army, and the South Sudan Army. We have an Armageddon. I am seeing everything that I saw in my dream coming to pass before my very eyes, and I know that my life and the lives of my people are in real danger, and only God is going to help us. My mother said to us run outside the city and lie down there. The guns were coming from both sides, and I was looking at the sky, and it looked like the rain of fire. We went outside the city and lay down, but the sound and seeing people getting killed was too much to bear for me. I got up and ran to the Nile River, but it was even worse there, and the sky was turning dark. My dad and the other men were fighting to defend us, but there were so many soldiers from South Sudan and North Sudan armies. I realized that life truly belongs to God, for we have no power to save our lives from this war.

A week later, the war was done, and we went back to our cities. And we had nothing, but we were very happy to be alive. In April of

1985, my family and I began to recover from that painful war. And our people were with us, and we started to worship God, and I said to myself, if my dream came true, is that vision of the four winds that I saw before that will come true too, and what will the four winds mean?

In September of 1985, my dad was working on his farm, and he heard his hand and he was feeling sick, so he went home, and slept in the afternoon. But earlier last month of August 1985, I saw visions about some men coming to our home, and I felt so scared. Every time I looked at my dad, I would only see blood on him. That has been going on for a month. But in September of 1985, my dad woke up from sleep and went back to his farm to care for the cows and other animals there. , and my mother, sisters, brother Moses Buay, and our grandmother stayed home, and my mother was cooking dinner. At about 6:pm on that day, Mom said to us let me go and told Paul that it was time for dinner. So she left, and then I saw 20 men with guns coming to our home, and they picked up my sister Sarah Nyapak Duer, and when I saw that, I screamed very loud, and I began to run, and then some of the men pushed me, and I felt down, and they punch me with the bottom of their guns, but I get up, and went through their legs, and begin to run crying. My father and my mother heard the loud noise that was coming from our home, and they were coming. I met them on the road, and they asked me what was going on and why are you crying. I said to them there are a lot of men at home, and they took Sarah, and they have guns. When my father heard that, he began to run, and he met my 9-year-old brother Moses Buay Duer, and he said to him dad, do not follow them. They have guns. My dad just began to run and follow them, and my mother went after him. Me, Grandma, Moses, and my little sister Maratha were at home. About 20 minutes later, we heard a gunshot, and my heart began feeling sick. I remembered the visions that I saw about my father being full of blood. I thought to myself, could they be true? At home, we were waiting, and we had no idea what was happening there with Dad, Sarah, and our mother. About 15 minutes later Mom, and Sarah come, and we don't see Dad with them. Now it is about 8:pm on September of 1985, and then my grandmother asks my mother where is my son. And My mother began to cry, and then I knew then that my dad was gone. But I was feeling like I was having a dream I don't believe that it was really happening. An hour later, people who heard the sounds of those guns' fire came, and they went to where my father was and carried him to our farmhouse. And some of them went after those guys, but they didn't find them. The next morning, the whole community heard what happened to my dad, and they came to see him where his body was at our farmhouse. My 9-year-old brother Moses and my 12-year-old sister Sarah went to the farmhouse too. But I didn't want to go, and I was still feeling shocked, and I could not believe that my dad was really gone. My father was a good man and a good teacher for the whole community, and many people are missing him. he was the backbone of our family, and we lost him.

One week later, those guys who killed my father, Paul, came back and took my sister Sarah, and my mother went to seek justice, but people came and said that they saw our mother with the South Sudanese Army with her hands tied up behind her back, and then they think that she was killed. I just turned 7-year-old, and my 9-year-old brother Moses and my 3-3-year-old little sister Martha are now left alone without anybody who can take care of us. Our lives are now turned upside down, and I realized that my life will never be the same anymore. I began to take care of my little sister Maratha, and I could not even hold her on my lap or pick her up because she was too big for me. to make things worse, I could not cook because I was just turning 7 -year-old, and I never try anything like that before. My mother's father was the one who always cared for us, and only Sarah, who is 12 years can help now, but those guys who killed my dad took her. Our father, who was in the same city as us, did not want to take care of us. I ask people for water and food, and sometimes they don't, and sometimes they do. I always make sure that my little sister Martha eats first before me and my brother Moses eats or drinks. Life as we know it was gone for us. I didn't really know anything yet about life, and I had no idea who should I blame for what had happened to our family.

The 1st miracle.

The Army took my mom, Mary, to jail and beat her up daily, and they set a date that they would kill her. About three months later, my mother had a dream the day before her execution date. In the dream, God said to her Mary, do you know that tomorrow is your execution day? Mary replied yes, I know, and God said to her why are you not afraid? Mary said to Him because I don't care now whether they kill me or not, I was seeking justice for my husband and my daughter, and this is what they done to me. Then God said to Mary, you have three small children who are suffering now, and no one is taking care of them; what will happen to them if they kill you, too? What their lives will be like? Listen to Mary tomorrow morning when you get up, go to the guard, and ask him to let you talk to the judge, and tell the judge that you were just seeking justice, and you have three little children who are left alone, and no one taking care of them now, and you want to go back, and take care of them. The next morning, my mother, Mary, woke up and did exactly what God had told her. She went to the guard of the South Sudanese army jail in the city called Bilpham and asked him if she could talk to the judge. The guard said to my mother it's very hard, and they never allow anyone to talk to the judge, but he says to Mary to wait for her. About 5 minutes later, the guard came back with the judge, and the judge asked my mother, what do you want, Mary? Today, I will hang you. My mother replied, I am just seeking justice for my husband who was killed, and those who killed him took my 12 years daughter Sarah, but now I have to go back home to my three kids that my husband left me because there is no one taking care of them now. The judge said to Mary, alright, this is the deal. I will send you home with my Army, and you have to give them 7 cows, and if they find out that you don't have 7 cows, they will kill you right there in front of your children. My mother said to the judge, my husband left 7 cows for me and my children, and I will give them to you. So my mother, Mary, and the soldiers leave for home. There in the city, we were struggling, and I did not know how long we were going to take it. One morning in December of 1985, I saw my mother coming, and I got up and went to her. The Army was with her, and I could not believe that she was really her; it felt like she had just come back to life. My mother picked up my little sister Martha, and my brother Moses was there, and we felt so happy. My mother gave them the 7 cows, and they left us with our mother. I asked my mother where is Sarah? and say to me she was not with me, so I came back to take care of you. But 2 years later, in 1988, a Nuer judge from Ethiopia called Mark Chuol Jock took the case and brought my sister Sarah back to us, and I was very happy to see her again. I am thankful to God for that first miracle that He did to bring our mother and our sister back to us; even though Dad was gone, we began to feel like humans again.

My Mother Mary Story:

My mother, Mary, got married at the age of 17, and then she realized that she had a gift of prophecy, and then people came to her seeking help from sickness and other problems. Then Christianity came to South Sudan, and she was feeling sick herself, and then she asked her husband, and said to him, I want to join this religion called Christianity, and her husband said okay. So, my mother started going to church, and she began to feel better. In the Nuerland in the 1960s, there rose a prophet, and many people were going to him. Prophet Tungkuach Bangong was telling Nuer men to bring their young women so he could test them by punching them on their stomachs while they were pregnant. Then, one day, Mary was called by her husband, and he said to her, I don't want you to go back to that church anymore because I was told that it's a true worship, and men are going there to look for women. Mary replied, but I asked you before, and you said it is good for me to join the church because you know how sick I was, and now I am well after I joined the church. Why now do I have to leave the church? What those people tell you about the church is not true. The next Sunday, Mary got up and went to church; when she was done, she left the church and walked home with her mother and other people. and then she saw her husband and his friends coming to her, and they began to beat up Mary. They were saying to her unfaithful wife, why you didn't listen to your husband when he told you not to go back to that church? But the next Sunday, Mary woke up in the morning and went back to church. After church, on her way home, she met her husband and his friends again coming to her, and they beat her up and said to her, never go back to that church again. No one is helping Mary, and two days later, Mary was called by her husband, who said to her Mary, I am going take you to prophet Tungkuach, and he will test you by punching you on your stomach, and if you don't die, and then I will know that the child you are pregnant with now is my baby. So he took me, and she was punched by the prophet in her stomach, but she didn't die. then he brought her back home and said to her, Mary, I still don't want you to the church. But Mary goes to church, and her husband and his friend meet her on the road, and they beat her up, and people say to her Mary, you have to leave the church or go to your father's house; these men will kill you. then Mary picked up her younger son, who was in her stomach when she was punched by false prophet Tungkuach Bangong; she left and went to her father's home and stayed there. then she went to church and met my father, Paul, there, and they fell in love and got married. then my Sister Sarah Nyapak was born, my brother Moses

Buay was born, and I, Nyajesus, was born, my younger brother Rout was born, and then my little sister Maratha was born. My little brother Rout died at the age of one, and I was too young to remember him; I was only two years old. My mother, Mary, left her other four children with her ex-husband, and he was taking care of them with his new wife. Mary loves my father, Paul, very much, and he loves her so much, and he treats her like a queen. Mary forget the bad life that she had when her ex-husband and his friends beat her up. Life is now wonderful with her new husband, Paul, and their children. Every week, Mary and her family go to church, worship God, and come very happy. Sometimes, Mary's other children come, and Paul loves them very much like his own children. But when they grow up, they begin to hate Paul. They say that he took their mother away from them, and then Mary and Paul tell them that it was a problem between Mary and their father about the church, and it has nothing to do with Paul, but they don't listen. In September of 1985, my stepbrothers and their friends, 20 of them, came to our home and killed Paul, who loved them very much and always gave them whatever they needed. In 1988, when Sarah came back to us, my mother Mary asked me, and said to me, Nyajesus, would you forgive your stepbrothers for killing your father Paul? I said to her, now I am only 9 years old, and when I turn 16 years old, I will kill all of them because they took my dad, who I love very much, and destroyed our family; I will not forgive them. So my stepbrother was watching me growing up and was very afraid of me, and people who knew my father, Paul, always said that I looked just like Paul, especially my teeth. then, the time was coming closer for me to be 16-years-old, and at the age of 14, my stepbrothers gave me in marriage to a 50 years old man who paid them many cows and money to take me, but I said no, I didn't want to get married or go to a far country, I want to stay close to my family. But they forced me to go, and they took me to Addis Ababa, Ethiopia, and I said to them that I was not going to that man. They say to me we know your plan, and what you will do when

13

you turn 16. Before I turned 16 years old, God asked me, and said to me, Nyajesus, what would you gain by killing your stepbrothers? Your dad will come back because you killed them, and others will come to kill your brother Moses Buay if you kill them, and I don't think that you want that. Then God said to me, Nyajesus, I am God, and justice belongs to me, and I want you to forgive your brothers. I said, but God, my heart is broken for what they have done. then He said to me, remember that I am God, and judgment belongs to me, so let it go, be free. I was thinking about it until I turned 16 years old, and once I sat down, prayed, and said okay, God, I will not harm my brother; I forgive them. But my brothers want me gone, so they still want me to go away to that 50-year-old man, and they beat me up every day. I say if they want me to be a woman at this very young age, I have to marry a guy who is close to my age. So I met a guy, and said to them let me marry this boy who is closer in age to me, and he will take me wherever he wants. then they went and asked people about the boy, and the people told them that the boy was a very bad guy, he would treat her very badly, and he was going to Canada soon. One of my brothers called me and said to me that we want you to marry that boy; it's fine with us if you don't want that 50-year-old man.I was very happy to hear that, and I thought that they meant it. So they gave me to the boy, and life was good for a month, but then the boy began to drink and beat me up.

The 2nd miracle.

And then I find out that I am pregnant, and my life turns from bad to worse. I am now 16 years old and have no family, and the father of my baby beat me up. I didn't know what to do or where to find help. then my baby was born, and for the first time in my life, I was a mother at the age of 16, and I had to take care of her alone in a place where I had no job. Life was very hard for me, but I still trust God. Every day,

I prayed and asked God to be with me through my life struggle and give me strength, and I hope, and I believe that I will make it, and one day my life will be better. At the age of 17, I gave birth to my son, but before he was born, his dad and I were told to wait for a latter from Kenya, and maybe we would go to Canada. So every day, the guys go to the mail box to see if we have that letter, but they always come back with nothing. then, one day, they get a letter that says that the man who was supposed to come with them to Canada had an H.I.V., and only you, Nyajesus, the daughter, and the dad must wait and see if you will go to Canada or not. So we waited and waited, and one day, the father of my daughter said to me, come with us to the mailbox, and then I went with them, and there was nothing there in the mailbox, and then we went back home. something interesting happened; the man I was with said to me Here is the key to the mailbox; the guys and I are going somewhere. I was so amazed because he had never given me the key before. then I took the key, and they left. I was at the house alone at about 4:pm, and then took a Nuer Gospel songs book and began to sing, and about 10 minutes later, while I was singing, something happened. I was feeling sleepy, and I could not move, and then I realized that I had a vision, and then I looked, and saw a yellow envelope, and I heard a voice which said to me take the key, get up, and go to the mailbox, so I get the key, and I get up and go, but when I was walking I cannot feel my feet touching the ground, and it same like the people don't see me walking. I got to the mailbox, opened it and saw the yellow envelope; I grabbed it and I began to walk back home, but I still could not feel myself and then I got home, went inside the house, sat down, and then I feel myself again, and then that when I really begin to understand what has just happened to me, and I begin to feel so happy and jumped up and said yes we are going to Canada, thank God we are going to Canada. The people hear me, and they come and say to me why are you dancing? I said to them because we are going to Canada, and then they said to me how do you know that?

I replied I went to the mailbox, and I got this yellow envelope, and that's why I am dancing. then they said to me but Nyajesus, you did not open the envelop yet for you to see what it said. I said to them yes but I already knew what it said, and it said that we were going to Canada, and then I turned, and saw the guys coming, and I started running towards them, and then I said to them, we are going to Canada they said to me how? and then I said because after you guys left me the key I was alone, and I take the Gospel song, and I begin to sing, and then while I was singing I went into a vision, and I see this yellow envelope, and then I hear a voice, and the voice said to me get the key, and get up, and go to the mailbox, and then I pick up the key, and get up, and I go to the mail box, I was still in the vision, and I feel like I am flying, so I open the mailbox, and I return back home holding this envelope, and I went inside the house, and sit down, and now I can feel myself again, and that I realize what was happing, and I begin to dance, and thanking God because for letting us past the test, and now we are going to Canada. then they took the envelope and opened it, and they later said, congratulations, you are going to Canada on November 17 1996. The guys could not believe it. then they said to me wow, how do you know what the letter said while you didn't even open it? This is a miracle, Nyajesus. God, hear your prayers. For all these years you have taken care of many people in your house while you have no job and no one who supports you, yet there was never a lack of food. You always gave them food and water. Nyajesus, God bless you, and now He allows you to go to Canada so you will have a good life there. then, the next day, we went to the Canadian Embassy and told them that we have another baby now, and we wanted you to ad him to the form so that he could come to Canada with us. But they say to us it is too late. Now, you leave in a month, and your form is complete, and we will not change it; if you want, we council your form because Nyajesus cannot stay here in Ethiopia with the baby and let Dilang go alone. We cannot separate the family; it is not our law. You have to leave the baby, and you, Nyajesus and Dilang must go to Canada. But I said to them my baby is only a month old, and I cannot leave alone. then they replied, there is nothing left for us to do. Your form is done, and you are going to Canada without your baby because we did not know about him. So we went back home and talked to our family, and they said that, don't worry, we will take care of him.

The 3rd miracle.

About a week later, the time came for us to leave Ethiopia and go to Canada, and we had no nice clothes or anything. The home we have been living in for one year, we had not to pay the landlord because we had no money. The people said to us there were 60. S.U.S. Dollars that we need to have you to go to the airport, and if you don't have them, they will not let you go to Canada. So Dilang begins to look for the money, but there is no one who wants to loan him the $60. S.U.S. dollars. I went and asked my brother to loan me some money so that we could have those sixty. S.U.S. dollars so that we could go to Canada, but my brother said no to me. Now, the day has come to leave, and we cannot leave without those sixty. S.U.S. dollars. In the afternoon, I was thinking about who I should ask for help now to give me the money? and then I said I am going ask my landlord to help and give me the money, but we hope the landlord will pay a lot of rent money how can he help us now? But I say my faith in God is strong enough, and I know that God will not let me down I will go to Canada. So I went to my landlord, and I said to her we were going to Canada today; she replied yes, thank God. I said to her, but there was a problem; she said why? I reply, because we need to have sixty. S.U.S. dollars for the people at the airport to let us go to Canada. And you know very well that we don't have money, and that's why we have not paid your rent for one year now. And we are very thankful for your kindness, and now we are going to Canada, and we will pay the rent amount that we owe you in full. So now I am asking you to please loan me money that equals the amount of sixty. S.U.S. dollars so that we can go to Canada, and then we will find jobs and pay you back everything we hope I promised you. Then she said to me, my husband is at work now. He will come home at 4:pm and come back at that time. So I went home and waited. Then Dilang said to me, Nyajeus we are not going to Canada because I cannot find anyone who is willing to loan me some money. I say to him God has been taking care of us for all these years, and I believe that He will let us go to Canada. So it's 4 pm now, and then I go back to the landlord, and I see that they are cooking, so I sit down, and then the woman landlord tells her husband what I told her, and I see him opening his wallet, and he takes some money out, and give them to his wife, and his come to me, and she gives them to me. I cannot believe it. I got up, and I thanked them and ran home, and I said to Dilang, I have the money, and we are going to Canada!, and then Dilang said where did you get the money? I say to him, I ask the landlords, and they give me the money. The guys were there, and other people, and they were saying to me, Nyajesus, it's a miracle. So Dilang left and went to get the sixty. S.U.S. dollars. Then he came back with the money of sixty. S.U.S. dollars and we went to the airport, but at the airport, no one asked us for any sixty. S.U.S. dollars, and we go into the airplane, and after 6 hours we land in Germany, and we have to wait there for 7 hours, and now we have to use these. S.U.S. dollars to buy food and water. God is magnificent, and that is when I really get the reason why we need to have the sixty. S.U.S. dollars because if we do have them we would have no water and food to eat, and we have a one-year-old baby girl with us. This is an amazing miracle. After that, we got to Canada, and I was so happy. Then, one month later, Dilang found a job in Canada, and we sent our landlords in Ethiopia all the money we hoped for them, and then we sent money to the people who take care of our baby in Ethiopia.

In Canada, Dilang has a family member, but I don't have any family members in Canada, and life is not going well for me because I am still getting beat up, and I cannot get any help because I don't speak English, and we are living now in Toronto ON, Canada, but in 1998 we moved to Calgary AB, Canada where Dilang uncle and his family live. My life is still not better, and I am being abused every day, and I still have no idea where to find help. then, one day, Dilang went out with his friend and drank, and I had a bad felling, so I took all the knives and hid them. At about 12:am, he comes home and knocks on the door. I wake up and go, and I open the door, and then he asks me who has been home with me today; I reply, no one, and then he pushes me, and he runs into the kitchen for the knife, but there is no knife there because I hide them earlier. then he came back and hit me in the face, and I fell down, and he began to kick me and push me, and he was saying to me, if I have a knife now, I can kill you. then I asked him why do you hate me so much; what did I do to you but giving you children? and then I push him back, and I get up, and open the door, and run upstairs, and I knock on doors but no one coming out to help me, and I begin to cry very loud, and then this couple opens their door, and they see Dilang coming to me, and holding something he grabs my cloth on my back, and push me downstairs, and I fall down on my face, and Dilang starts beating me up, and then these couples help me the lady call the police, and the man was saying to Dilang, you are not a ma why are you doing that to your woman. But Dilang was crying, and he was asking where is the knife that he could kill Nyajesus now, but he didn't know that the police were coming; then we heard a sound, and the police came and pushed him away from me, and they picked me up, and take me inside the car for the hospital, and then they take me, and they put Dilang to Jail. This couple even takes care of my two children until I come back home. About a month later, we went to the court, and the couple came to have my witnesses and the judge wanted to put Dilang in jail and stay there. But I say no, let him go. these couples were very sad to hear that, and they said to me, but Nyajesus, he almost killed you; just let him go to jail. But I cannot explain my reason why I want him not to be put in jail because I don't speak English. So the court let him go, and I go home with him. then Dilang was still beating me up and did not want to call the police. So, I started going to school to learn English, and I began to understand some of the words in English, but that was not enough because I could not really speak it. then, one day, the child welfare came and told us that we heard that you had been fighting, but Nyajesus had not called the police, and now we will take your children. then I said to them, do not take my kids away from me. They reply, but Nyajesus, you don't care for your life whether this guy kills you or not, and what would happen to these small children who will take care of them? Well, now you can stay here with him, and we will take your children. I called the Nuer community leader, and he came and said to child welfare that I would not take the kids. I will take care of them, but they said no, we cannot leave without the children. I cried and cried, but they did not listen to me. Then they took the children. My son was only one year old, and my daughter was 4 years old. then the police who came with them took me to the hospital because they thought that I had lost my mind. But the Dr. checked me, and let me go home. I was feeling so terrible, and I was now missing my two small children, and I had no idea how I was going to get them back. I start going to kung Fu after school. about a month later we go to court, and they let us see the children every two weeks; every time I see my kids, I feel so happy, but when they leave, I feel so sad. Life become very hard for me. Every day, I pray to God and ask him to let my children come back to me and lead me in the right direction. At Dilang, still abusing me, I have nowhere to go, and I really don't care about me getting hard; all I want is my children. About 6 months later, we went back to court, and the judge said to me I am not going give you the kids back because you are very young to take care of them, I replied to him and said, but God gave them to me, and I love them, and that's why I have been taking care of them since they were born. He said again to me but Nyajesus, you have been abused for four years now, and you never call the police or get some help. I say to him it's because, in my culture, we don't just leave the man whenever he treats us badly; we think that is not good. So that's why I stay with this man for so long, and I need my children I cannot live without them. The judge said to me I would give them to you with a condition: if you get beat up again or if that man gets into a fight because he drinks, and I find out, and you did tell your lawyer, I will take your children, and you will get them back again. I said okay. So I get my children back and take them home. One hour later, I got a call, and the lady said, Nyajesus Dilnag got into a fight, and the police are taking him to jail now. I said thank you for telling me because if he gets there, and I have not let my lawyer know about it, they can come and take my kids, and I will not get them back. I hung up, called my lawyer and told him what happened, and he said to me, Nyajesus, you did a good thing because if you did not call me now, and the judge finds out, your children would be taken away from you, and you will not get them back again.

The 4th miracle.

So I made a decision to leave Calgary and go back to ON Canada, where I first was since I came from Ethiopia. About a month later, we went to court, and I needed full custody of my children and the judge gave it to me, and I went to the welfare office and asked them to pay for my family's airline tickets, but they said to me we don't pay for the airline tickets only bus tickets. I said to them we could not take a bus in the winter, and the journey was three days. I don't speak English, and there are so many different buses to take. My son, who is 2 years old, has Asthma, and he will get sick on the way, and no one will help me. The lady who was there at the office said to me, we want you to go to your Dr and let him write a letter that proves that your son is sick. So I said okay, we left, and I went to the Dr. he wrote a letter that my caseworker thinks is very good, and then we came back to the office, and we gave it to them, but they said to us this later is not enough to give you an airline ticket. My caseworker was very helpless, and I didn't know what to do. We go home, and then we come back to them again, and we ask them to rethink their decision because I have no other options. Then they say to us we will let you meet with the manager; wait here. About 10 minutes later, the manager came, and told us the same thing, and he said we have been telling you, we do not pay for the airline tickets; it's our law. I turned around and saw my caseworker, and she was looking so sad, and then the manager got up and went to the window of the office. I lifted up my head and looked at the sky. I prayed to God and said to him, God, you are the one who brought me here to this faraway land where I have no family, and I don't even speak the language, yet you have been taking care of me, and you have given me back my children, and now we are free to go back to ON, Canada where the man who knew my father lives with his family, and he wants to help me when I get there. While I was in prayer, the manager came back, sat down, and began to write on his computer, and he said to us, you are going to ON, Canada, on February 14, and then; when my caseworker heard him saying that she jumps up with joy, and she saying to me Nyajesus did you hear that? I turned to her and said yes, I hear that. But I know that what was happening was a miracle for God just changed the manager's mind, and it's so amazing. So, on February 14 / 2000, my small children came back to ON Canada, and I was feeling fabulous.

Where did the Nuer people come from?

Nuer has a unique history, which began with the creation of the world; that's when all human beings were only in the form of one man, Adam and one woman, Eve, in the book of Genesis, chapter 1,2,3. But at the fall of man in Genesis 3: when they ate the forbidden fruit and were told by God to leave the garden of Eden and went to live in the place outside the garden, and then they began to have children, which the first was Cain and Able. And so has the history of human beings keep moving on from the family of Adam and Eve to their descendants. and in (Genesis 10:6-20) Ham, one of the three sons of Noah whom God saved during the great flood that was in Genesis 6, has four sons: Cush, Mizraim, Put and Canaan. And these nations who came from Ham, three of them live in Africa, and the fourth of them, who is Canaan, lives in his Land, Canaan, which we call today Israel. But the question is, where is Canaan today? This is a very good question indeed because all the nations in (Genesis 10:) are all known today, and we understand who they are except Canaan, son of Ham. The history was told of a people called the Israelites who came from Abraham; they were told by God to go and destroy the nations of Canaan and take their land. But the real story has never been told until now. The Hebrews were and are the same has the Canaanites. Abram, who was told by God to leave his father's house and go to a land I will show you, is none other than a Canaanite whose family moved from Canaan to Babylon, which is also inhabited by Cush; he was also a son of Ham. The kingdom of Babylon was founded by the son of Cush,

23

who is called Nimrod, and Abram and his family lived in Babylon before God spoke to him and told him to leave his family and go to Canaan. It is never God's will to take land from other people and give it to another person who doesn't have the right to that land. This history, which has been told to us that the Israelites were a different people apart from the Canaanites, is false and should not be regarded as a true history at all, for this happened to let the world forget about the real people of the land and their real history. The true history is that all the children of Ham have lived in the so-called Mid-East and in Africa since the beginning of the world., and the Canaanites, who are also the Israelites, went to Africa because other nations came and took their land, and it is also the same of the Cushite who are now called Ethiopian who was in their land of Babylon but left and went to Africa because their land was taken by other nation. The Nuer people are the Hebrews and Canaanites who journeyed from their land of Canaan to Egypt and lived with the Egyptians for a long time and even ruled. One of their son, who was a great leader in Egypt, was King Tut. The name Tut is only found in the Nuer men in Africa; there are thousands of men in the Nuerland who are called Tut today, and this is a fact. In the history of mankind and the table of the nations in the book of(Genesis 10:) God makes it very clear who is who and where those nations live according to their territories, and there is no question about who werethe sons of Ham and where they live today. Their lands are not as big as they were, but they are mostly in Africa and also all over the world because of slavery. So, the Nuer people were also called Anglo Egyptians from 1899 to 1956 by the British. The history of the Nuer people has been lost for centuries until now, and the Nuer or Naath people only know their short history, which began when they came to Sudan and settled in the area we now call the Greater Upper Nile region and also another area. But their true origin is that they came from the land of Canaan, and they are the true descendants of the Hebrews and the Canaanites. and many of them are all over Africa and also throughout the world. In the Book of (Isaiah 18:) and the Book of (Zephaniah 3:10), God has identified them very clearly and has a say in what would happen to the Naath / Nuer people in the last days. They would live with other sons of Ham until they got their land of Canaan back. Their history was told by their prophets who wrote the Bible and also their other prophets who rose up in the land of Sudan, and they continued their way of life as it was when they lived in their land of Canaan. The Naath or Nuer people believe in God, who created heaven and earth, and they keep the laws of Moses and make sacrifices just like the way they did in their land of Canaan. They are a very peaceful and loving people because of their culture and they have been living this way since their beginning. Many people have joined them, and they also became one with them because they love the way Naath or Nuer people live and how they let all people live freely and according to their own way and understanding of life.

Where did the Dingka Tribe come from?

The Dingka tribe are from Mizraim or Egypt, the second son of Ham. The Dingkan or Mizraim always live with his youngest brother Naath, Canaan or Hebrews, known as the Israelites because they are close to each other and their lands are sometimes united as one nation. This still continues even today; they always regard themselves as one people. In the history of the Bible (Genesis 10:6-20), God talks about the sons of Ham and their lands, and we understand that all of the sons of Ham live in what we now call the Middle East and also in Africa. The land of Canaan or Israelites is what we now call Israel; the children of Canaan are not living now there in Canaan or Israel because they were pushed out of their land by those other nations. Mizraim was in his land of Egypt until 1899, when the British came and took over, and the Arabs also came and lived in the land with them. In 1956, when the British ended their rule and Sudan became independent, Naath and Dingkan were a part of that new nation of Sudan. But these two tribes, Naath and Dingka was, in a fair relationship until the coming of the British and the Arabs in the 18th century when they began asking themselves about what to do about the British and the Arabs who were invited to their land and taken over their rules. The Naath or Nuer people told their brothers, the Dingkan, that it would be great for us to welcome the Arabs in our land instead of the British because, in the future, our children could fight the Arabs and get their independence back, but they would not be able to defeat the British in the future and they not get their independent back if we allowed the British to stay in our land. But the Dingkan said that they wanted the British and not the Arabs to stay in their land. That was the beginning of the long separation between these two tribes in their views of how they should live in the land and others. Even when they got their independence from the Arabs and lived in the nation of Sudan and the British left them, they were still now in harmony with each other. The Naath people went their own ways, and the Dingkan went their own ways. They also lived in different territories, and even their languages differed. The Juba conference in June 1947 was no different; the Naath Nuer and the Dingkan were still not agreeing on how the situation of those other people, namely the British and the Arabs, should be dealt with. In the 1960s, when the Southern Sudanese tribes began to unite themselves and wanted their own independent nation from the Arabs in the Sudan, that also brought the attention between the Naath people and Dingkan, and through their struggle of seeking their own independent nation in the Southern Sudan, the Naath wanted a full and a free nation, and the Dingkan wanted a changed and united Sudan. That kept going on and on until 2011, when Southern Sudan became an independent country from Northern Sudan, which was ruled by the Arabs. That same to be a very wonderful idea, and it looks like the Naath and the Dingkan would finally be living in harmony. But in 2013, that dream was crushed when the Dingkan government ordered a door-to-door killing of the Naath people, and the new country of Southern Sudan went into a horrible civil war that's taken seven years and even now that I am writing this book in 2020 there still no real peace in Southern Sudan. And has a child who is a survivor of this regime. I still think that there is hope for our tribes to live in harmony as we sometimes did in our history in the land of Egypt and Canaan, and we should really go back in time and understand how our people began and their journey into these other lands and that we are and always will be the children of Ham and we shared this wonderful land and even our children and their children will be here in this land,

and we must learn to love one another and know that we are truly one family forever. This is the dream and hope of the many people in South Sudan to be able to live together in harmony without any trouble and share all the resources of our land with peace. And we should focus on building our nation, which is really in great need of development in the world. We are the youngest nation and poorest nation in the world, and we should put all our attention on the betterment of our country and make it one of the best nations in the world. This is not new; every nation has gone through some sort of trouble in the beginning, and the only difference would be how soon we can start doing the good things instead of the bad things.

Who were the Hebrews Israelites?

In the history of the Hebrews in the Bible, God told of their begging from Abram, who was in the land of Cush with his family, and God called him out of there into a land he will show him the land of Canaan, but what we don't understand is that Abram was no other then a Canaanite himself who his family earlier moved from Canaan into the land of Cush Babylon. God didn't call Abram a foreign into a known land. No, he already knew that Abram belonged to that land of Canaan because God found him a righteous man among his people who were living in the land of Canaan and also his own father's house. It was God's plan to start a new nation of Canaan from Abram because he was not pleased with how the Canaanites were living, and it had something to do with how they worshipped God. Abram was a perfect human like Noah, who was keeping the laws of God and living well with his people of his generation. And so, the Hebrews were born when Abram obeyed the voice of the Lord God and went back to Canaan and started his own nation, and his descendants became the Israelites, but their origin is from Canaan. It is how the human race is. They always reinvent themselves into a new nation and a new people, nothing new at all. In the book of (Genesis 37) when Jacob, one of the grandsons of Abram, was living in the land of Canaan with his family and his elder sons sold his younger son Joseph into slavery in Egypt and Joseph became governor in the land of Egypt during a great drat, so, Jacob his father sent his brother to Egypt to get some food for them, and Joseph saw his brothers and knew who they were, but his brothers did not know who Joseph was. Joseph refused to give them food, and he told them to go back to Canaan and bring their youngest brother, Benjamin, and so they did. Then Joseph revealed himself to his brothers, and his brothers went back to Canaan and brought their father, Jacob, to Egypt. they lived there in Egypt until the birth of Moses and the Exodus when the Lord God told the prophet Moses to Pharaoh to let his people go to serve him in the wilderness of Sinai. The Canaanites became the Hebrews or Israelites, and they lived in the land of Canaan many times, but they always sinned against God, always resulting in them being taken into slavery by other nations. So, the Naath people are the Hebrews Israelites who are scatted throughout the world in slavery, but God has promised that he will gather his people in the last days and bring them back into their own land, the land of Canaan, and he will bless them and be with them and so the nations will know that he loves them and have returned to be with them forever more. That's why Naath Prophet Gnondeng Bong prophesied that the Naath people would have peace at last. He was not only talking about South Sudan's independence but a new nation that would be born and which all his people all over the world would come and live in peace in their own country, the land of Canaan, .God's will be finally realized on earth. For all nations will go to seek God on Mount Zion, the high hill of the most high God of the Israelites, and then there will be an everlasting peace through out the whole world. Joy, peace and prosperity will cover all nations, and all people will praise God forever.

Who was the Canaanite who lived in the land of Canaan?

The Canaanites came from Ham son of Noah. The history is told in the Bible that Noah had three sons, Japheth, Shem and Ham, and Noah was told by God in (Genesis 6:) to build an Ark to save his family and the animals for God was sad that he had created mankind because their thoughts are only evil always and he wanted to destroy every living thing on the face of the whole world. And so, Noah, the only righteous man in his generation obeyed God, and he and his three sons built an Ark and were saved from the great flood and to repopulate the whole earth. And then, after the great flood, God made the rainbow covenant with Noah that as long as the rainbow appears in the sky, God will not bring rain again to destroy the world. So, his sons went to their territories and began to build their own cities, but one of the greatest known was Nimrod, the grandson of Ham, who started his Kingdom of Babylon in the land of Shinar and told the others to join him in the building of that giant call the tower of babel in (Genesis 11: 1-9), God saw what they began to do and came and confused their language which is GEEZ, and scatted them throughout the earth. And Canaan, son of Ham, founded his nation and he named after himself the land of Canaan, and his descendants lived there in their own land. There were 12 nations who lived in Canaan: the Canaanites, Perizzites, Hittites, Jebusites, Amorites, Girgashite, Hivites, Arkites, Sinite, Arvadite, Zemarites and Hamathites. All those nations came from Canaan, son of Ham, and they are the ones who are named the 12 tribes of Israel who were living in the land of Canaan when God showed his love and his mercy to Abraham and saved the people of Canaan by giving them a new faith in God who always lives in Salem (Psalm 76:2) or mounts Zion the city the great king Melchizedek the high priest of the highest who was a Jebusite, a Canaanite king, and the new testament says that Christ is a priest according to the order of Melchizedek. (Psalm 110:4) (Hebrews 7:3) So, as we can see now, the Hebrews Israelites are the same as the Canaanites, and that's why the Bible calls them the 12 tribes because that what they are from their beginning and forever, and we have to realize that they are not lost but scatted all over the earth through slavery for disobeying God. This has happened many times throughout their history, but God always forgave their sins and brought them again to himself, for they are his chosen servants forever, and their land of Canaan is the holy land of God forever more.

In the book of (Zephaniah 3:9), God says for I will restore to the peoples a pure language (Geez), that they all may call on the name of the Lord Yecu, to serve him with one consent. The name Yecu came from the name Yah, YHWH. Psalm 68:4. God of the Hebrews the Canaanite. God wants his people to remember his laws and return back to him, and he will give them pure language, and God will be with them forever. The sons of Ham have been put down as nothing because of the false history that was created that Noah cursed his son Ham because he looked on him when he was sleeping and naked, and Canaan, the grandson of Noah, was cursed by Noah. But that's not true at all because the real history is that, before the flood, God gave a special covering to Adam when he was kicked out from the Garden of Eden, for God created him to be a king over the earth. And when Noah was found righteous in his generation by God, God gave him the holy covering to protect him in the Ark. And so when the flood receded (Genesis 8:3), Noah and his family went out from the Ark and began to live on the earth again, and one day Noah was sleeping, and the holy covering was on him, and his three sons was outside the tent. Noah's elder sons are Japheth and Shem, and Ham is the youngest

32

son. Has we all know, the elder son always gets the firstborn promised, but not so with God. God only deals with the faithfulness of a human heart. So, God has chosen Ham, the youngest son of Noah and his son Canaan, to carry out his holiness throughout the world, starting in the land of Canaan and the Jebusite city of Salem that became known as Jerusalem, the city of the great king and high priest of the highest God Melchizedek the Canaanite. And that's why when Ham's brothers saw him with the holy covering, they went and told their father, Noah that Ham took his holy covering while he was sleeping. But Noah did not curse Ham; he blessed him and his son Canaan to be the holy people who will live in the holy land of God, and all the nations will come to their land and worship God in Salem or Zion. Ham brothers Japheth and Shem would share in God's divine work and blessing on the earth. That's why there are seventy nations in the Bible, and they are all one big family who came from their beloved father, Noah, who was a righteous man who obeyed the voice of the Lord and built an Ark to save his family and the animals.

When did the Arabs come to Egypt and Sudan?

The Arabs first came to Egypt and Sudan as missionaries in the 16th and 17th centuries. They were called Sufi holy men; they came to spread the Islamic religion mixed with the African traditional beliefs and customs. Many Nubians who lived along the Nile River followed their teachings and the missionaries instilled a deep devotion to Islam that was not there before. They built schools and taught the people until the end of the Egyptian-Ottoman rule. In July 1820, Muhammad Ali had victory over Egypt and the Ottoman Empire, and he sent an army under his son Ismail to conquer the Sudan. Muhammad Ali was looking for the gold and the slaves that he would find in Sudan and to be able to control the whole land, which he did in 1821 when some of the tribes who lived along the Nile and Atbara rivers and the surrounding regions surrendered. That's when the Naath and Dingkan tribes were trying to find a way to deal with the Arabs and the coming British, and there was a lot of disagreement between them about who to welcome to stay in their land of Egypt and Sudan. The Dingka tribes wanted the British to stay in the land, while the Naath people wanted the Arabs to stay in the land. That disagreement has never been solved, even today, and it is the real cause of the problem in South Sudan and the war between Naath and Dingkan. And the only way to overcome that is to go back and learn their history, and where they came from and how they lived before those other peoples came into their land and divided them; that would be a wonderful thing, and that would bring a new thinking and a new change would come and maybe they will reunite and live peacefully together again and build their nation.

When did the British come to Egypt and Sudan?

In January 1899, an Anglo-Egyptian agreement restored Egyptian rule in Sudan but as part of a joint authority exercised by the United Kingdom and Egypt. The agreement designated territory south of the twenty-second parallel as the Anglo-Egyptian Sudan. Although it emphasized Egypt's indebtedness to Britain for its participation in the reconquest, the agreement failed to clarify the juridical relationship between the two condominium powers in Sudan or to provide a legal basis for continued British governing of the territory on behalf of the Khedive. Article 11 of the agreement specified that" the supreme military and civil command in Sudan shall be vested in one offer, termed the governor-general of Sudan. He shall be appointed by Khedival decree on the recommendation of her Britannic Majesty's government and shall be removed only by Khedival decree with the consent of her Briitannic Majesty's government. The British governor-general, who was a military officer, reported to the foreign office through its resident agent in Cairo. In practice, however, he exercised extraordinary powers and directed the condominium government from Khartoum as if it were a colonial administration. Sir Reginald Wingate succeeded Kitchener as governor-general in 1899. In each province, two inspectors and several district commissioners aided the British governor (mudir). Initially, nearly all administrative personnel were British Army officers attached to the Egyptian Army. In 1901, however, civilian administrators started arriving in the Sudan from Britain and formed the nucleus of the Sudan political service. Egyptians filled middle-level posts while Sudanese gradually acquired lower-level positions. And that is how our land of Egypt and Sudan was taken by the Arabs and the British. How great it is to know the history and really understand what happened so that we can truly move on and find our way back to how our lives were before they came into our land. That is the great quest of our people.

Who are the sons of Noah?

The sons of Noah are Japheth, Shem and Ham, and the Bible makes it very clear who they are and where they live, even their descendants. In Genesis 10, God gives us the table of the nations who came from the sons of Noah. Japheth, the firstborn of Noah, after the Great Flood, moved to the upper northern part of the world and also to the east part of the world. His descendants are all listed in Genesis 10, and there is no question about who they are. God calls them the Gentile nations from their father Japheth line. The sons of Japheth are Gomer, Magog, Madai, Javan, Tubal, Meshech, and Tiras. Genesis 10:2-4. All Japheth descendants are now called European and Asian. Shem is the second son of Noah and his sons are Elam, Asshur, Arphaxad, Lud and Aram. They live in the land we now call Arabsia, and they always have many in counters with the sons of Ham because they live very close to each other and their lands are very close. Ham is the 3rd son of Noah, and his sons are Cush, Mizraim, Phut, and Canaan. And they live in their lands close to each other. Cush, the first son of Ham, lived in Babylon, which we now call Iraq, and he later moved from Babylon to Ethiopia, where he lives now. Mizraim, the 2nd son of Ham, lived in the land we now call Egypt, but he was later removed from his land by other nations, and he now lives in South Sudan. Plus, the 3rd son of Ham, lived in his own land we now call Somalia. Canaan, the 4th son of Ham, lived in his land, Canaan, but was scattered by other nations, and he is now all over the world and in South Sudan. And this is the history of the sons of Ham and their lands. Has we can see, the whole world is one BIG family that came from one creator, and we should not hate each other; we should know and understand that even if we look different, we are still one people, and we should love each other and treat each other with respect and honor. The world belongs to us all, and we are here to stay, so let's make it better.

The Naath religion.

The Naath religion is one of the most well-known among the African religions and in the world. When the Naath people left their land of Canaan and went to the land of their brother Mizraim or Egypt, they were still keeping the laws of God, who was given to Moses on Mount Sinai. After the journey from Egypt to Sudan, the Naath or Hebrews Israelites, had many prophets who were prophesying about what would happen in the future. One of the well-known prophets was Ngundeng Bong, and after him, his son Guek who was a prophet too. The Naath people are very religious people, and they love to worship God and do everything according to God's will. Other tribes in Africa love them for their devotion to God and their respect for others and life itself. But that kind of lifestyle they did get when they moved to Africa. They have lived that way since their founder in the land of Canaan. Throughout their history, they always believed in God and followed his ways, and that's the core of their culture. Melchizedek was king of the city of Salem in Canaan. The city was renamed Jerusalem by King David, a Hebrews and Canaanites. Naath or Hebrews history is mankind's history, and all nations are welcome to worship the God of Abraham, who is the God of Noah and Adam and Eve. Prophet Ngundeng Bong prophesies just like the other prophets before him, like Isaiah, Daniel, Malachi, and so many other prophets who wrote the Bible, and they all were talking about God's will for his people and the whole world. His divine promises to all mankind that one day they will all live in peace with each other, and that will happen because God will raise up a great leader from the Israelites who will bring all nations together, and they will worship God on Mount Zion or Salem.

When did Christianity come to the Nuerland?

The missionaries came to the Nuerland in the mid of the 19 century, and they thought that these people had no idea about God, but as they began their teaching about God's salvation to mankind, it all became clear that the Nuer people already knew who God of Israel was because it is their God who spoke to them on mount Sinai when Moses took them from the land of Egypt to Sinai. But the only one issue was the man Christ who they said died for their sins, and they most believe in him for God to forgive their sins. That was a very BIG problem because they always bring sacrifices to God according to the Laws of God that he gave to Moses on Mount Sinai. The belief in God was not new, and the idea that someone would come and bring people closer to God was already there in the Nuer culture, but the point that a leader already came and died for their sins was just unbelievable. So, they saw Christianity as a different religion, and must still worship God the way they already had for centuries, but because the Nuer are very peaceful, they did not want to make the missionaries feel bad; they were still sharing the word of God with them and welcoming them into their homes. The Naath language is very easy to learn, so some of the missionaries learned the Nuer language very quickly, and they are communicated very smoothly with them. and many of those missionaries stayed with the Nuer people for a long time. their names and stories were always told to the new generation of the Nuer people. The missionaries did a very big study about the Nuer and their culture and also their religion and they came to the term that the Nuer beliefs

41

and culture were really related to the Israelites of the Old Testament, and the only question was why? They didn't understand how the Nuer people would know so much about God when there were no missionaries that had been there in their land before. But the truth of the fact is that the Nuer people are the Israelites who came from the land of Canaan and went back to Egypt because their land was taken by other nations, and they always go to Egypt whenever there is a problem in the land of Canaan. The Naath or Nuer people journeyed to Sudan in the late of the 19 century and lived with their relatives from the tribe of Mizraim or Dingka. The Nuer people still believe in God just the way they always have since they were in Canaan, and they know that some of the teachings from the missionaries are not in harmony with the teaching of the laws of God in the Old Testament, and they have been focusing on the study of the prophecies of prophet Ngundeng bong and the old testament prophets to find out the truth about God's word in the last days about them and also for the mankind. The Naath people welcome other people's opinions and they are not worried about their beliefs in God because they know that it is God who knows everything about all human beings and how they can find salvation. So, in the Bible, like Isaiah 18 and Zephaniah 3, they talk about the Naath people living in a land divided by two rivers, which are the white Nile and the Blue Nile, which are located in Ethiopia and Sudan. And God says that the Naath or Israelites will bring gifts to Mount Zion in the last days. It also says in the book of Zephaniah 3:10 that from beyond the rivers of Ethiopia, his worshipers, the Naath, will bring offerings. So, then the question becomes, what are the gifts that the Naath people will bring to God on Mount Zion? And also, where is Mount Zion? We all know that the land of Canaan has been taken by the Gentiles, who are also claiming to be the people of God and Nuer people know that South Sudan is the homeland that God brought them to live in, and God has not told them to return to the old Canaan land in the Middle East. This is a very interesting situation for the Naath people, who are also the Hebrews, and God has given them a big task to do in these last days. They are to bring God's gifts to Mount Zion. And now, they are waiting for the Lord's direction to Zion and his revelation on where is Mount Zion and who or what the gifts are that they are supposed to bring to Him. But the Nuer faith in God is very strong and they know that God will reveal that to them when the time comes, and there is no doubt about it at all. Many people are talking about the lost tribes of Israel, and some of them are claiming to be them, but this is not a game to God. It is very important to really identify who are the tribes of Israel who are also descendants of Canaan, son of Ham. As I clarified before, the Hebrews Israelites were the same people as the Canaanites, and there was just a name change ordered by God to Abraham because of the sins that the Canaanites were doing against God by worshipping other gods in the holy land of Canaan. So, God gave them a new beginning through Abraham, who was also a Canaanite, so that God forgave their sins as a nation with a new name and faith. Also, God changed his name from El to YHWH so they could believe in only one God, who is the God of Abraham.

The God of Abraham, Isaac and Jacob became YHWH; we call him in the Naath language Y.E.C.U. It is the same name in the Hebrew language because the Naath language is still close to the Hebrew language. In all human history it is very common for people or a nation to change their identity and give them a new name and even a new God, and that's exactly what happened to the Canaanites who became the Hebrews Israelites. We, the Naath people, were called by that name in the 18th and 19th centuries, but we are now called Nuer people, and this name became who we are called today all over the world. But a long time ago, we were called the Jebusite from Canaanites, and we lived in the holy city of Salem with our high priest and king Melchizedek. And then, we were changed and became the tribe of Judah from the Israelites. This is our history, and we are very grateful to God Most High for his grace and protection over our people, for giving us this knowledge and understanding about our history and for revealing his excellent salvation to us and also to mankind. I am writing this book to clarify the confusion about who Nuer and Dingka are, not only in this century but in the past. Our history has been hidden for a long time but now is being revealed to the whole world because it is the Lord's will that we would so journey into all the world, and in the last days, we would come back to our God, and he will guide us and bring us back to our true origin from the begging of the world. Our father Ham was cursed by Noah but blessed by Noah. Canaan is blessed, and he was given God's inheritance as the youngest son of Ham because his father Ham took the holy garment from Noah that God gave to Adam from the Garden of Eden. That holy garment was the one who protected Noah and his family in the Ark during the great flood.

Kingdom of Canaan, the United Afro-States story

In 1895, Menelik II went to Wech Deng in Nuerland to seek help from the Nuer prophet Ngundeng Bong Chen Makuch Jockroal chaany. Emperor Menelik II was going to war with Italy, and he needed help. The prophet Ngundeng Bong gave Emperor Menelik ii a cow bull called Tungkernyaang, but Prophet Ngundeng Bong cut the tale of the Tungkernyaang and prophet Ngundeng Bong wanted the relationship between Sudan and Ethiopia to last forever, so Emperor Menelik ii married Nyayan Ker Makuach Jockroal Chany. They had a son and called him Tungkernyaang, after the cow that was given to him by prophet Ngundeng Bong. Emperor Menelik II left wech deng with the cow Tungkernyaang with the blessing from prophet Ngundeng Bong. Emperor Menelik II went to war with Italy in March 1896 and won the war of Adwa. Emperor Menelik II, after the war, agreed that his son Tungkernyaang would be in South Sudan.

Tungkernyaang was raised by his uncle Wol Ker Makuach Jockroal Chaany in Nuerland. When he grew up, his uncle went to Egypt to look for tools for his garden, and on his way home, he found a girl name Nyeguol Yor, and he wanted Tungkerynaang to marry her. So he talked to Nyeguol's father Yor about that and told him, give me your daughter Nyeguol, and I will give you the tools that I brought from Egypt; I want my sister Nyayan Ker Makuch Jockroal Chaany son Tungkernyaang Menelik II to marry your daughter Nyeguol Yor. And then Yor agreed, and Tungkernyaang Menelik II married Nyeguol Yor, and Tungkernyaang and Nyeguol Yor had a Son, and they named him Kok because his mother Nyeguol was brought by the tools that Tungkernyaang Menelik II's uncle Wol Ker Makuach Jockroal Chaany brought from Egypt for his garden, and they have another two children who are girls and name them Nyalual and Mear. Kok Tungkernyaang got married to a Nuer girl called Nyebol Dhol, and they had children: Nyaliew Kok Tungkernyaang Menelik II, Deng Kok Tungkernyaang Menelik II, and Paul Duen Kok Tungkernyaang Menelik II.

Paul Duen Kok Tungkernyaang Menelik II married Mary Nyagony Deng, and they have children: Sarah Nyapak Paul Duen Kok Tungkernyaang Menelik II, Moses Buay Paul Duen Kok Tungkernyaang Menelik II, Rebecca Nyajesus Paul Duen Kok Tungkernyaang Menelik II, Ruot Paul Duen Kok Tungkernyaang Menelik II, and Nyabel Paul Duen Kok Tungkernyaang Menelik II. In 1982, Paul Duen Kok Tungkernyaang talked to his children and told them the story and said that, Prophet Ngungdeng Bong and Emperor Menelik ii wanted to set up God's kingdom on Mount Zion, The New New Jerusalem or Bilpam, because through Nyayan Makuach Jockroal Chaany and Emperor Menelik ii's son Tungkernyaang, now Nuerland became the holy land, and the Nuer people are now the new Isreal. In 1974, the Ethiopian Solomonic dynasty came to an end.

Emperor Haile Selassie (I) and Ethiopia's 225th and last Emperor were overthrown by Mengistu Haile Mariam. From 1974 and now, the only place for the Solomonic dynast is in Nuerland. And in 2012, the Kingdom of Canaan, The United Afro States, was founded, and Queen

Nyayecu (I) is the head of the kingdom. Rebecca Nyajesus or Nyayecu Paul Duen Kok Tungkernyaang Menelik II is qualified to rule in the Name of God because she is the direct descendant of King Solomon and King David of Israel through Emperor Menelik II and his only son in Nuerland Tungkernyaang. God or Deng, through Prophet Ngundeng Bong, gave Emperor Menelik II the power to win the war of Adwa, and he did. Nuer people and black people in general now have a God's Kingdom, which is the Kingdom of Canaan, The United Afro States. All the slaves all over the world who were taken from Africa and the people who were left in Africa are now one in their Kingdom of Canaan, The United Afro States.

Kingdom of Canaan, The United Afro States Capital city, is Mount Zion, The New Jerusalem, or Bilpam. It was prophesied by the prophet Isaiah in (Isaiah 18: 1-7) that gifts would be brought to Mount Zion by people who are tall and smooth skinned people. God is talking about the Nuer people, and the gifts are the slaves who were taken from Africa during the slave trade. God now wants them to return back to their people and their kingdom of Canaan, The United Afro States. It was also prophesied by prophet Zephaniah in (Zephaniah 3 10), which says beyond the rivers (White Nile and Blue Nile) of Ethiopia my worshipers Nuer people, the daughter of my scattered people, will bring my offerings.

The daughter here is Nyajesus or Nyayecu Paul Duen Kok
Tungkernyaang Menelik II. That's why when She was born, her family
knew that she was the promised one who was to come, and they called
her Nyajesus or Nyayecu, which means the one who will save her
people and the anointed one. Queen Nyayecu was chosen by God to
restore God's Kingdom, the Solomonic dynasty, which was destroyed
in Ethiopia in 1974. Nyajesus has children: Nyahook, Mandella,
Buomkuoth, Joy, Moses, Sarah and Malachy.

And her man is the honourable the great. He is one of the ministers in The Kingdom of Canaan, The United States, Bilpam or Mount Zion, The New Jerusalem. Gooybank is located in Mount Zion, The New Jerusalem or Bilpam.

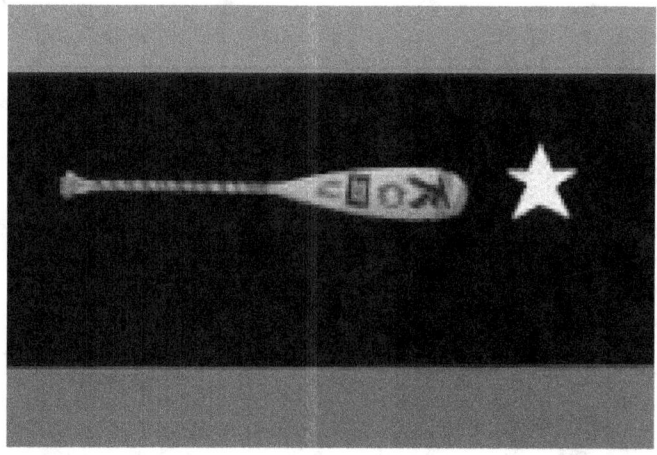

Ngundeng Bong says good things and bad things; never will my flag mix with Roal or goyim's flag, the God who brings thunder to the world. Let's go and see that coming star. Tell Doal Juong that I am just going to find food, not to stay there forever. The false prophets will be shaken; the whole World will be shaken. Raw maanyang, I will make a dusty wind. Makuach comes beautifully. I will welcome you. Power cannot be with one person forever, even if he can turn the world around. Jocknyeal that its horn touches the sky.

Written by Queen Nyayecu (I) June 11, 2015.

Gooy Bank Global Central Bank history

Gooy Bank Global Central Bank belongs to the Absolute Theocratic Monarchy by the divine right of kings, the Kingdom of Canaan United Afro States Southern Sudan Wakanda and Ben Kuara Kuoth God's Coming Kingdom International. The Imperial Davidic Solomonic Dynasty Sudanese Branch was started in 1896 by Prophet Gnungdeng Bong Makuach Jockroal Chaany from the Jikieny Nuer

Tribe of the Greater Upper Nile Region of Sudan and Emperor
Menelik ii of Ethiopia. Prince Paul Duen Kok Tungkernyang Menelik
ii and Her Imperial Majesty Queen Mary Nyegony Deng's reign began
on February 15/1972. Prince Paul Duen Kok Tungkernyang Menelik
II passed away on Sept.12/1985, and Queen Mary Nyegony Deng
passed away on May 16/ 2022.

On June 6/2022 Rebecca Nyajesus Duen Kok Tungkernyang
Menelik ii reign began as Her Divine Imperial Majesty Empress
Nyayecu, Queen of Kings elect of God of the Kingdom of Canaan
United Afro States Southern Sudan Wakanda, The Divine Absolute
Theocratic Monarchy of the Imperial House of the Davidic Solomonic
Dynasty by the divine right.

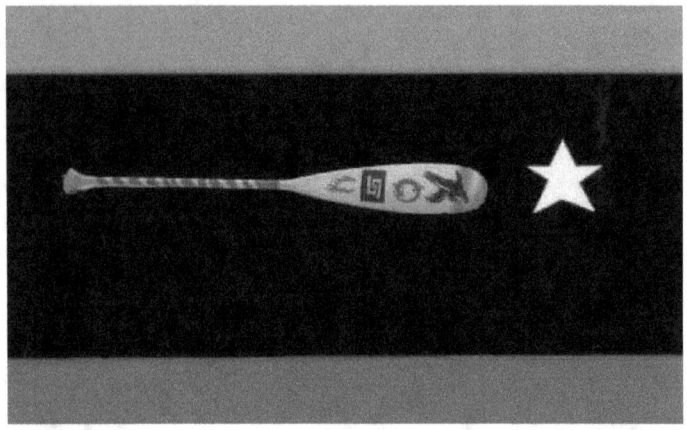

Gooy Bank Global Central Bank Headquarters in the Greater
Upper Nile Region and in Gambella, Ethiopia... E.O.C.E.O. is now
Bishop James Gatluak Nyak Kuel, his Voice President Rabbi Simon
Gatluak Kun Deng, and the Bank Manager Moses Mayan Tut Put. The
Royal Family of the Kingdom of Canaan United Afro States Southern
Sudan Wakanda the Davidic Solomonic Dynasty Theocratic Absolute
Monarchy Net worth is $900.6 Billion Dollars in 2023 from lands, oil
and investments. Phone number: +251901940665. Email Address is:
gooybank@gmail.com / nuerbank@gmail.com

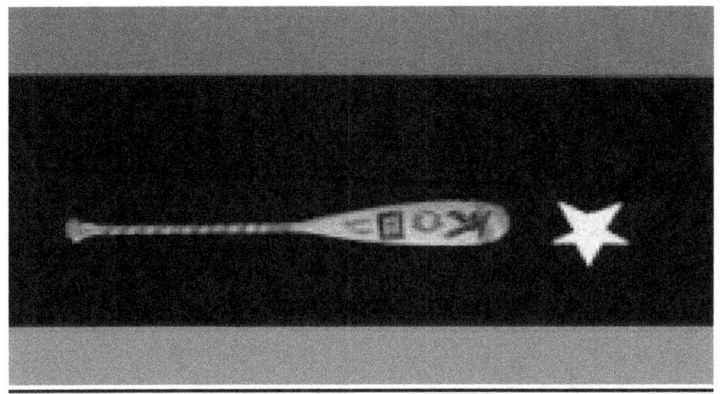

The Afro Covenant:

Canaan, The United Afro States.

One nation, one currency, one language and one Army.

Article 1.

Canaan U.A.S. includes all African states that are in Africa and also in the Caribbean.

Article 2.

All the heads of the states of afro nations are now members of the board of governors of Canaan U.A.S.

Article 3.

Canaan U.A.S. is a theocratic government based on the Afro priesthood, and all the governors must learn Afro religion, history, past, present and future. And they must love and care enough for all African people and they must know and respect God.

Article 4.

This afro covenant must be signed by the head of the state and ratified in 30 days.

Article 5.

We all Afro people under this covenant have one head of the state, who is God. The high priest, the governors and the people. God is our ruler and his word is law.

Article 6.

Has one nation, one government, one currency, one language, one Army and one people.

Article 7.

All Afro people are free to travel throughout the U.A.S. The Afro people who are outside Africa are now free to come back home to Africa and they can choose any place to live in Africa. If they want to become citizens of the U.A.S., they are free to do so. All Afro people, no matter where they were born, can become citizens of the U.A.S. if they want to.

Article 8.

The judges of the U.A.S. must be people who know and understand the laws and customs of Afro, and they must respect them at all times.

Article 9.

There must be no foreign that can become the head of the judges or president of the U.A.S., And they must not be part of the Afro supreme council or priest.

Article 10.

All citizens of U.A.S. must know and understand the laws and afro way of life and culture, and they must respect them always. They must respect the high priest's words and they must know that the words come from God.

Article 11.

U.A.S. is governed by God's laws and the high priest. The governors are the heads of the local governments, but they share the same laws with the central government.

Article 12.

The U.A.S.A. deals with the central issues, but the U.A.S.P deals with the local matters.

Article 13.

U.A.S. has a supreme court and the local courts that deal with local matters.

Article 14.

U.A.S. must not look for advice outside our nation, and we must deal with our own matters. And we must not seek help from any foreign nations.

Article 15.

Has a nation, we must know and understand that our God is with us at all times.

Article 16.

All Afro heads of the states must know and understand that, by signing this Afro covenant, they are now and forever bound by this covenant and they will not leave this union.

Article 17.

All citizens of the U.A.S. have the right to buy and own land anywhere in the U.A.S. and their children have the right to live with them or become a new owner of their family's land.

Article 18.

The people who work in the government must do their jobs with knowledge and understanding of the Afro culture and costumes. And they must never disrespect the rights of the U.A.S. citizens.

Article 19.

The first priority of those who work for the people of the U.A.S. is to love, respect, care and provide for all citizens.

Article 20.

In the U.A.S., our citizens' needs and wants come first before ours. All the people of the U.A.S. must be taken care of at all times.

Article 21.

We have one people and nation; we must have one love, one voice and one vision. Our future is one.

Article 22.

For a violation of this covenant, there will be a penalty. We must always remember.

Article 23.

This political unification is final. And because it's coming from our creator, it must last forever. We have a people who must love one another and care for each other at all times because we are one people.

Article 24.

All the resources of the U.A.S. belong to all the citizens. We must respect the ownership of land by family. The government must not take what belongs to citizens.

Article 25.

In the U.A.S., we use only the U.A.S's gooy currency. That's our national currency that's most used to buy goods and services throughout the land.

Article 26.

We, the people of the U.S.A., must love and respect anyone who lives among us, and we must care for them.

Article 27.

We, has one people, must worship only one God and show love for one another. We must not show any violence at all times. Only love, peace and joy to one another.

Article 28.

We, as people who most respect the elderly people, young and children, must be taken care of at all times.

Article 29.

Our central government most deal with other nations. And the local governments most deal with local matters. And the local government most not make any deal with other nations.

Article 30.

And because we have one Army that deals with central issues, the police are the ones who deal most with and take care of the local matters. And there must not be a divided army in the U.A.S.

Article 31.

We only recognize the marriage between a man and a woman in the U.A.S. according to God's laws.

Article 32.

We, as a citizen of the U.A.S. must take care of our land and nation. And we must take care of our people. We must know and understand that this is our homeland forever and we must treat it with love and respect.

Article 33.

We, as citizens of U.A.S., most love and respect our leaders because they are here to care for us and God will bless our nation if we love one another and respect each other.

Article 34.

We, the people of this nation, U.A.S., are one. If something happens to one state of the U.A.S., it's our thing, too, and we must deal with it together as one nation.

www.ingramcontent.com/pod-product-compliance
Lightning Source LLC
Chambersburg PA
CBHW070939120626
46546CB00004B/1474